Her Bare Soul:

Poems from an African American Woman's Perspective

Jalissa Monique Brown

Contact:

Email: jalissabooks@gmail.com

Twitter: @sexywomenread

 Instagram: @sexywomenread

Facebook: Jalissa Brown

#HerBareSoul

Her

Bare

Soul

Dedication:

For those who love the skin they are in and for those who are learning.

With much love,

Jalissa Monique Brown

Poems by Title:

Baring her soul became her therapy in the form of prose...

Her Bare Soul

Take a deep, long look within her soul,

Her bare soul,

Scars remain

With undertones of unrecognizable colors.

Vibrant colors of laughter and happiness

Once filled the lines of a place she held so dearly,

Now what's left is emptiness,

Ready to be filled again.

Dear Hispaniola

It is well documented when the first slaves arrived to the land,

Sweat and blood filled the cracks of a nation that's now divided into two, all because of one command.

Intentions were to assist the Tainos, but the impact had a greater cost,

A long legacy of pain and a complete culture lost.

Encouragement of inferiority because of color and creed,

All for sweetness of cane left a lifetime of bitterness derived from greed.

A legacy built on that same sweetness left such a bitter taste,

For once, instead of seeing skin color, could we imagine seeing God's face?

For it is written that we were all made in his image,

Despite desired or forced, all of our ancestors have made some type of pilgrimage.

Caged Black Bird

She goes to her most sacred place,

A place where only her heart knows

And searches for a pen,

With the pen she bleeds from her soul

And reminisces of a love for a black bird,

A caged black bird.

Her spirit awakens

As she thinks back to when she first saw the caged black bird,

He wasn't just any type of black bird;

He was the true definition of a bird,

King of the sky.

See, this black bird was not always a caged black bird,

He once soared across the skies of the concrete jungle.

When he flew by,

The other black birds would gaze at greatness

Right before their eyes,

The black bird would sing his song as he passed them

And from that moment, the other black birds felt great too.

They only felt great for the moment

Because part of the earth

That rotates on a mentality of stereotypes

Released hate into the atmosphere,

Which then becomes self-hate.

A feeling of inferiority

And unworthiness.

Those are the very reasons why this black bird,

The true definition of a bird,

King of the sky

Was taken from his tree and caged.

Taken because some of earth's other creatures feared him.

The darkness of his feathers

And beauty in his wings

Was often imitated.

They robbed him of the fruits of his labor,

Deprived him of the seeds he had sown,

Underestimated his intelligence,

And loathed when he survived.

The song that he sung every morning did not sit well with them.

The lyrics of his song

Went against their brainwashing agenda

That everything the black bird stood for was bad.

His song spoke of self-love

And black bird greatness,

Which was often misconstrued.

Believing in the greatness of black birds

Didn't mean all birds didn't possess that same greatness,

The black bird felt he just needed to sing his song

A little louder.

He sang so passionately that he was indeed a black bird,

but simply a bird as well.

Despite the opinions of the other creatures,

She saw the good in him,

but the black bird saw things she never understood,

Sorrow had completely filled his eyes.

He knew he was an endangered species,

He knew they wanted him caged,

Wiped out.

Caged because part of the God-given earth,

Couldn't appreciate the value of the black bird.

They comprehended the value of the black bird

But wanted to hinder the value

From influencing the other black birds

That they too were king of the skies.

Could it be a fear,

A fear of potential,

Or were they threatened by black bird's greatness?

She began to cry,

She cried because his offspring will never see him soar above the

concrete jungle.

Her love for the caged black bird runs deep,

So deep that the earth could never convince her that her beloved,

The caged black bird

Is anything less than great.

She finishes the letter

And seals it with a kiss,

In hopes it touches the beak of the black bird,

The same beak

That sang of the black bird's greatness.

Marvelous Creation

Every part of you

That I discover daily

Is like the Almighty Creator had searched the very nooks of my

imagination,

And so carefully placed you in my life.

As I entered the gallery of love,

I immediately noticed God's artistry.

I became amazed at how he took broken pieces

And crafted you in his own image,

A portrait worth loving,

A dark and mysterious painting worth admiring,

You're a marvelous creation.

I saw what others couldn't see;

The beauty in your flaws filled my eyes.

The wall that I had built over my heart

Had been bare for a while;

I had learned to embrace the bare wall

Because I was promised one of God's most marvelous creations

To fill that very space.

Thank God for saving his greatest work of art

Just for me

In the form of you,

A marvelous a creation.

Black Queen

Queen you are,

Chosen the color black.

Black because you were meant to beat the odds,

The odds of light shining from your darkness.

Queen you are,

Chosen the color black.

Black because you were meant to be different,

Different enough for everyone else to stare in awe.

Queen you are,

Chosen the color black.

Black like ebony,

Strong in nature,

And some may even have undertones of beautiful chocolate
cosmos.

Queen you are,

Chosen the color black.

How magical and magnificent it is

To be from such a culture

Of resiliency

And beauty.

Queen you are,

Chosen the color black.

The Berry Picker

The berry picker searched for the darkest berries,

They sold better at the market.

He was known to have the darkest berries.

He sold them proudly with the slogan,

"The darker the berry,

The sweeter the juice".

He sold them faithfully at the farmers market for years

And people came from miles away

Just to get his berries.

He took pride in their appearance

And their sweetness,

For he knew the worth of the darkest berries.

Freedom

Autumn leaves fell

And chatter amongst the students filled the hallways,

Study groups were formed

And lunch dates were planned.

Greensboro,

A college town was painted with every walk of life,

There I sat at a tofu lunch counter

In the heart of downtown.

I was accompanied by

One Asian, two Caucasians, and one foreign exchange student,

We ran down the list of things we all had planned to attend

together,

It was freedom

That was fought for not many decades ago,

And it was freedom

I felt as I ate my tofu at that very lunch counter.

Black Renaissance

Rebirth of a mindset that you too are great,

Poetry, new dance moves, music, and other arts filled the streets

of an uptown neighborhood.

With heads held high,

We all now walk the streets of what became known as the Black

Mecca,

What a feeling

To be part of a people who went down in history as literary and

artistic greats.

Talent filled the air beyond the rooftops of the high rises and

closed the gaps of not fitting in,

Now,

there was value put on the lives of skin that look like mine.

Intellects from all walks of life took notice to the light that

shined on the darkest of them all,

There was a movement towards empowerment and redefining.

Black,

Reborn.

Yes, that's me!

Sandy

There stood a beautiful beach front property,

Decorated with a façade of a great relationship,

There was a constant struggle to sweep sand from the hard wood floors

And to continue pushing ill emotions underneath the Welcome rug.

Delicious aromas from the taco shack

And sea salt with a sunscreen mixed concoction filled the air.

Views of bleached hair, darkened skin, and sun-kissed lovers with no end

Gave the final touches to this scene.

It wasn't until October,

One stormy day

That the truth shattered that beach front property

In the form of a mighty storm.

Water filled the space where the lies once roamed,

The hurt and the pain quickly tried to stay afloat

Where they once resided.

Then came that final wave,

It wiped away what once stood

As a beautiful beachfront property.

The façade of a great relationship

Had washed away at sea.

Star

Out of all the stars in the sky,

You were the one

That gave me that twinkle in my eye.

Your best attributes

Form constellations in my heart,

Filling it with a light so bright

It warms the very depth of my soul.

At Sea

A dark cloud of disappointment

And precipitation of pain

Poured directly on me

As I stood there looking up to the heavens

Seeking guidance.

A storm of heartbreak

Was coming in my direction

To overthrow me

And to destroy

The very ship I built

To protect my precious cargo.

A cargo filled with hope,

Desire,

And a dream that one day I would find the treasure,

The treasure in a co-caption in this voyage of life.

Through the storm,

You appeared

And I immediately raised the white flag.

I surrendered.

In the midst of the storm,

It was evident

That you were the one

To battle the waves of life.

Brown Sugar,

You, my brown sugar

Was wonderfully made,

Every grain of you

Was carefully envisioned

By the almighty God.

He took his time

And went the extra step

Of refining exactly what he wanted you to be.

He saw the creation of something beautiful,

He saw you, my brown sugar.

He made you extra sweet,

With a different kind of taste

To ensure that the world knew

That you, my brown sugar was set apart.

Set apart with a purpose

Of adding a flavor in everyone's life that you meet.

You, my brown sugar, Stay sweet.

Sister

Programmed

By a society to upkeep the revolving door

Of being each other's competition,

It remains as a constant reminder

Of the brainwashing that occurred long before us.

Allowing our physical features

To be compared

Instead of the intelligence

And power we share,

A complete lack of trust

And respect

Continues to roam the air in which we breathe.

The captor's plan continues to succeed.

I lied.

Their plan has superseded their expectations.

We failed.

We failed our ancestors.

See me as your sister,

A way the captor's never wanted.

Let us hold hands tightly

And use our forces together

To push down that revolving door,

For together

We are stronger.

Together

We are one.

Mississippi

Darkness settled on the Mississippi,

The thick blanket of resentment dressed as fog

Made it harder for the man in the boat to steer.

The man was new to the river,

Never set foot in her waters before,

She took note to that

And made it even more difficult for him to know of her curves

And the highs and lows of her waters.

She forced her waters against his steering

Hoping the more force she used

The more he would give up.

She tried to destroy him

Before he could conquer the heart of her

And the very center of her flow.

She broke through the levees

That held her sanity intact.

There was a rising of her waters from deep within

Leaving her soul

In a state of emergency.

In the midst of her unsteady waters,

The man in the boat remained persistent

And displayed a genuine desire to wait,

to wait out her flood of emotions.

He did so without any worrying

Of the damage his boat might incur.

She tested his will

Once again

By trying to force him overboard.

The man in the boat remained focused,

Dedicated to withstanding the unsteady waters

In hopes of her becoming calm.

The whispers of the river's heart

Questioned if the man in the boat would endure the ride

Until the very end.

Everyone called the man in the boat crazy

Because the Mississippi had all the signs

Of a flood of emotions approaching.

Despite what others said

And despite her troubled waters,

He knew

To travel her waters was a chance of a lifetime,

For she was like no other.

She was not only a river,

She was a great river,

River of all rivers,

She was the Mississippi.

Her Blues

Applauses filled the air as she graced the stage.

She looked in the eyes of those who filled the room.

She had waited her whole life for this moment,

A moment to share her blues.

It hadn't always been the blues;

It was once reds and blacks.

Those were the colors left from the blood stained sheets

And black was the color it left her soul.

Life was taken from her.

Scared,

Alone,

Confused,

She put it all in a song.

She added the red

To the black

And sang her blues.

Her Darkness Shines

In a world that perceives darkness as dim,

her darkness shines.

She has the power to light up nations

and to create greatness.

She lives in a world where being dark is unattractive,

yet her darkness is what makes her even more undeniably

beautiful.

Chestnut,

Caramel drizzles,

Even a mixture of mocha delight,

Is what makes her a sight to see,

She illuminates

The very world

That tries to convince her

That she's really dim since the very moment of her creation.

Her darkness shines.

Her darkness is needed

 For the stars to be visible.

The stars shine through her,

 Therefore

Her darkness shines.

Story Time

Her story

May not be my story

But together

It makes our story,

Which they call his-to-ry.

A history filled with tainted truths and backhanded praises,

When really it is to silence the voice our ancestors could have had.

So when you see me,

You're really seeing her,

And when you see her,

You're really seeing us.

Together we have the power to create our future,

Remembering the ones who paved the way.

They Never Said

They never said life would be like this,

Despite it all, being with you makes even the worst days feel like bliss.

From constant phone calls from debt collectors and threats of eviction

I continue to see the light at the end of this tunnel, I believe in us despite our current situation.

They never said finding a purpose after college would turn into a lifelong task,

Hiding emotions of failure, defeat and fear, I use my grand laughter as a mask.

But you know how I really feel; you're the one who wipe my tears at night,

You're the one that tells me to never give up and continue to fight.

They never said societal pressures would get worse the older you get,

Expectations of starting a family, building a house, and trying my best not to do something I'll regret.

The stresses of life often get me down and leave me with unwanted dismays,

But the fact that I have you by my side proves the sun will shine on the rainiest of days.

Office Horror Story

She walked down the office aisle,

Some began to stare.

It wasn't to look at her navy blue skirt

Or to watch as she redefined grace in four inch pumps.

It was to see through her.

A blatant attempt to find fault,

Incompetency,

And diminish her efforts.

Despite the stares,

She had a sway in her hips as she paced at the rhythm of her

thighs rubbing together.

Her presence was demanding

And even though she saw the stares,

She pressed her full lips together

And said hello.

She then stretched those same full lips to form a smile,

A smile so bright that it lit the entire office of negativity.

Some said hello back,

Some nodded,

Many held concealed weapons of fake smiles,

And others just waited.

They had been waiting for her to break.

Some thought to themselves, "There's no way she can keep it together when things got stressful".

"She's not capable of handling the tasks we should have been given,"

So they thought.

She knew they wanted her to act out of character

And to fulfill the role that they had given her in this office horror story,

Of the mad black woman.

Little did they know,

That wasn't the role she came to play;

She came to play a confident,

Outspoken,

And madly passionate woman

That happened to be black.

So as she walked down the aisle,

She thought to herself,

"let them stare"

And she hoped they enjoyed the plot twist

Of the office horror story,

Of a mad black woman.

White Dress With the Flowers On It

That day my mother didn't have to wake me.

I rose at the crack of dawn,

It was Easter Sunday.

No sleep in my eyes,

I hurried to get dressed.

I carefully removed the bonnet revealing my perfectly placed bun.

My toes wiggled in excitement at the sight of my dress.

See, the day before we had searched the city both near and far for the perfect dress.

We found the dress in the very back of a department store,

hanging and waiting just for me on the clearance rack.

I picked out the best dress of them all, the white dress with the

flowers on it.

As I hassled to put the dress over my head,

I dared not to misplace not even a strand of hair from my bun,

I twirled around and around,

 Feeling like the princess my dad had always told me that I was.

My mom stood at the door smiling and reminded me to brush

my teeth and to grab my bible.

We walked a few blocks

Then hopped on the bus.

We walked towards the back of the bus,

Straight to the colored section.

I took my time as I walked the aisle of the bus,

Acting as though it was my runway,

Showing off my white dress with the flowers on it.

Forbidden Fruit

We waited.

Under the stars,

We waited.

We heard the howling of the wolves,

We waited.

Mosquitoes bit at our ankles and crickets buzzed in unison

As though it was a symphony as the night fell.

Dogs that surrounded the Big House

Barked at the constant sounds of the frogs from the pound.

It was time.

Time to taste a fruit so sweet

It was worth dying for, it was a forbidden fruit.

Death or a beating close to death

Was the consequence if caught indulging in the fruit.

It was time.

Time to run,

Run for glory in hopes of reuniting with my love,

My brave love.

He had left a year before

But I knew once I got to the north

He would welcome me in open arms.

Life eating the forbidden fruit was worth the escape.

We waited.

I squatted even lower in the bushes,

 Hoping not to be spotted.

The forbidden fruit felt so close

 I could taste the sweet nectar.

I scratched at the welt

That was still fresh from two days ago.

 It was from hiding a pen and paper.

I had been practicing copying a letter

That I found in the trash.

I didn't know what it said

But I remembered every letter.

Once I got with my love,

I would show him what I had learned.

Thoughts of him

Brought a smile to my face,

And a calmness that started in the depth of my belly.

I looked up at the moon

Still thinking of my love

Hoping he too was looking up at the moon at that very moment.

The time came.

It was time to run,

Not just run, but run for life.

Run for a chance to taste the forbidden fruit, freedom.

Child

I apologize

For the current state of the very place God made for us to live,

You have shown me exactly how to love,

To you, my heart I give.

I hope you learn the most important lessons in life,

I want you to live a life of happiness

Without any strife.

I pray that each day that you wake

You know that you were wonderfully and fearfully made.

Thank you for allowing me to show you the way,

And forgive me for all the mistakes I've ever made.

I am far from perfect,

But God chose me to show you just how special you are.

My love for you is forever,

Even when you grow older

And whether you are near or far.

With every breath that you take,

Remember your skin is that color

Because that was the reflection of God's heart that day.

Having you as my child

Is the greatest gift of all,

The sight of your smile

Proves God's grace each and every day.

Her Bare Soul

"For she loves the skin she's in,

forever."

About the Author

Jalissa Monique Brown is a writer born and raised in North Carolina. She is a graduate of the University of North Carolina at Greensboro, with a Bachelor of Arts degree in International and Global Studies. She also minored in Political Science, while strengthening her language skills in Spanish and French. Her studies concentrated on culture and human rights.

Her small town roots inspired her to travel and see the world she always read about as a child. One of her first jobs was a library page at the Public Library in her hometown.

After graduating college she moved to New York City, where she now resides. She spends her time teaching English as a Second Language, traveling, reading many books and writing about her experiences. Her first published poetry collection is entitled *Live Life Loving*.

www.ingramcontent.com/pod-product-compliance
Lightning Source LLC
Chambersburg PA
CBHW061157040426
42445CB00013B/1708